My name's Holly and I live
on a hobby farm, which means
we raise animals for fun and
not as a business. We have
three goats, two horses, geese, a
rabbit, two cats, and a puppy.

The baby goats are named
Timothy and Tag and they're
twins. They like to nibble on
goldenrod, and sometimes I
take them to run in the meadow.

Goats can be milked just like cows. The only difference is that goats have two faucets instead of four. We milk Angel twice a day. The twins don't have any milk because they're both boys.

Goat's milk is delicious! I use it on my cereal in the morning. Goldie, who is one of my cats, likes it too.

One of our horses is an Arabian named Katrinka. We've had her since she was a baby. I'm responsible for feeding all the animals when I get home from school. Katrinka eats about half a bale of hay and five pounds of oats a day. Mommy feeds her in the mornings.

Sparkle is my second cat, and she and Goldie play together while I take care of my chores.

Timothy and Tag's mommy is named Angel and she's very well behaved when I give her a haircut. It's important to trim goats' hair often so they stay clean. It also keeps them cool in the summer. Daddy and I do this with electric clippers.

They live in a big pen and that's where they go
when they're finished playing. I feed them
hay for dinner.

My other horse is Melodie
and I'm learning to ride
her. Mommy holds a long
training rope called
a lunge line.

I named my rabbit Easter Bunny because my friend Wendy gave her to me as a present last Easter. Wendy brought her over to our house with a red ribbon around her neck.

She lives in a wire house called a hutch. If Daddy doesn't hold her when she's outside, she might run away or scratch me with her long claws. She eats carrots and alfalfa.

The geese act like watchdogs—they make
a lot of noise if strangers come on our property.
They're my friends because they eat the flies and bugs.

Bambi is the name of
the golden retriever puppy
I'm taking care of for
a year. Then she will be a
Leader Dog for a blind person.

I'm training her how to walk
on a leash and how to behave
herself in the house. That means
I don't feed her food from
the table or let her climb up
on the furniture.

We practice a few times a day
and she's catching on now.
But sometimes she leads me
instead of my leading her.

After we're through
with our lesson, we
have a nice tummy rub.

Down by the creek, there's a
forest of ferns where Bambi
and I play hide-and-seek. She
gets covered with burrs and
thistles, but I take them off her.

I help take care of the garden
in our backyard. I have my
own hoe to chop away the weeds.

We all love corn and so do our animals.
The horses like the long stalks, and the
husks go to Easter Bunny. If there are
any small ears, they go to the goats.

There's a big field of sunflowers near our house. In the winter we cut off some of the tops and dry them in the sun. Then the birds come along and pick out the seeds. Sometimes we roast the seeds for ourselves and they're delicious. Our neighbors harvest the flowers in the fall to make sunflower oil.

This year Timothy and I did something wonderful. We went to our first 4-H Fair. It lasted for a week and Mommy, Daddy, and I camped out there in our camper.

When you join the 4-H Club you make a promise which says: "I pledge my Head to clearer thinking, my Heart to greater loyalty, my Hands to larger service, my Health to better living, for my club, my community, my country, and my world."

At the fair there is lots to do. There are competitions for horses, dogs, pigs, goats, cows, sheep, rabbits, and poultry. They even have a competition for guinea pigs. They also award prizes to people who make things like quilts and pies.

We all give each other a hand
taking care of the animals.
I helped my friend Laura give
her pig Abner a bath before it
was time to show him. We used
baby shampoo instead of soap
because it's better for his skin.

Our Leader Dog Club made a big
puppy out of chicken wire, tissue,
and some brown carpeting. The
judges pinned a blue ribbon on him.

When it was time for the goat class,
Timothy and I were very nervous.
But the judge told us we were all doing
a good job. He walked over and checked
each goat for cleanliness and grooming.
Then we each walked around the ring so
he could see how we handled our goats.